Mommah NeNe's Place of Adventure

My Surprise Party

Copyright © 2022 by Shaneika Jacobs. 833522

All rights reserved. No part of this book may be reproduced or transmitted in any form or by any means, electronic or mechanical, including photocopying, recording, or by any information storage and retrieval system, without permission in writing from the copyright owner.

This is a work of fiction. Names, characters, places and incidents either are the product of the author's imagination or are used fictitiously, and any resemblance to any actual persons, living or dead, events, or locales is entirely coincidental.

To order additional copies of this book, contact:
Xlibris
844-714-8691
www.Xlibris.com
Orders@Xlibris.com

ISBN: Softcover   978-1-6698-0748-3
       EBook   978-1-6698-0747-6

Library of Congress Control Number: 2022901000

Print information available on the last page.

Rev. date: 01/14/2022

Mommah NeNe's Place of Adventure

Shaneika Jacobs

Mommah NeNe's Place of Adventures

Hi, my name is Unique. The name of my favorite place in the world to go is Mommah NeNe's.

It all started on my 8th birthday. I got a big surprise birthday party from Mommah NeNe herself. Mommah NeNe and all the other staff members picked me up caring me down the hall singing happy birthday at the top of their lungs.

Ms. Tammy was holding a birthday cake with a big number 8, my name and party streamers sticking out of the side. I had no idea what was at the end of that hallway but I was pretty sure it was the beginning of an amazing adventure.

There was a bright light coming from underneath the door. Ms. Tammy swung open the door. I was blinded by the bright light.

To my surprise there were 5 other children standing around with balloons, party streamers, party whistles and a very big pinata. My heart became overwhelmed with joy.

We played games like pin the tail on the donkey.

Limbo

Tug of War, scavenger hunt, musical chairs and what I had been waiting for the entire day "the breaking of the pinata".

This was the best birthday I had ever had. On my way home I told my mom the spectacular way Mommah NeNe and the other teachers had introduced me to my new classroom.

I told her how they picked me up and carried me down the hallway. I told her how scary it was and how the bright light blinded my eyes. I couldn't stop talking about all the exciting things I had done at my surprise birthday party. The more excited I got I began to look like I was conducting a musical. This was the most perfect way to get introduced to Mommah NeNe's classroom. But little did I know my introduction to the classroom was only the beginning of what would be an amazing adventure at Mommah NeNe's Place of Adventure.

CPSIA information can be obtained
at www.ICGtesting.com
Printed in the USA
BVHW021559220322
632091BV00002B/46